A Bruised Light

A Bruised Light

Pamela Portwood

A Bruised Light

Copyright © 2006
by Pamela Portwood

cover art by Hoge Day

cover design by Trisha Hadley

photo credit: Mark Taylor

All rights reserved. No part of this book may be used or reproduced in any manner whatsoever without written permission from the publisher, except in the case of brief quotations embodied in articles and reviews.

Published by

~Star Cloud Press~
6137 East Mescal Street
Scottsdale, Arizona 85254-5418

ISBN:

1-932842-18-7 — $12.95

Library of Congress Control Number: 2006921444

Printed in the United States of America

Preface

When I set out to write *A Bruised Light*, I began with a list of over 70 writers, artists, musicians, saints, philosophers, emperors, kings, scientists and other historical figures who were reputed to have had epilepsy. I had compiled the list from half a dozen books about epilepsy. I had intended to read biographies, autobiographies, letters and other material by those figures and their contemporaries to use as inspiration and sources for a series of poems about famous people with epilepsy.

Along the way, I discovered that some of the authors of the books on epilepsy had cited each other without having consulted any primary sources. As I pursued the primary sources myself, at times, it seemed that the mere mention of a "fit" or of a seizure in someone's death throes was enough to get a famous person on someone's list and so be carried forward, book after book, decade after decade. On the other hand, I am sure there are primary sources that I did not find because I did not want to do scholarly research; I wanted to write poems. Even so, I did far more research for *A Bruised Light* than I ever intended to do.

Two of the most interesting, informative and well-documented sources about epilepsy are *Seized: Temporal Lobe Epilepsy as a Medical, Historical and Artistic Phenomenon* by Eve LaPlante and *The Falling Sickness: A History of Epilepsy from the Greeks to the Beginnings of Modern Neurology* by Owsei Temkin.

Although many of the incidents that I relate in the poems in sections two and three are based on recorded history, there is great contention about whether some of these people actually had epilepsy. In some cases, I have chosen people who were diagnosed with epilepsy in their own time but have since been identified as having other medical conditions. A number of the poems in section two are about the figures' seizure experiences; others are about the people or their lives. Many are dramatic monologues spoken in their voices or in the voices of their contemporaries.

Section three concentrates on medical interpretations and treatments for epilepsy in different cultures and periods. Section one features personal poems. They deal both with my own seizure experiences and with the loss of cognitive and memory skills that were side effects of the first epilepsy medications that I took after I was diagnosed with epilepsy. Although my poetry has never been affected by seizure medications, at one point, my prose skills were so impaired that I had to quit working as a free-lance writer. I was lucky because new epilepsy medications came on the American market in the 1990s. Eventually, I was able to get my seizures under control with limited side effects, and I began writing prose again. When I lost my words, I lost a part of my self. There is no poem in here to express the return of my very self. There should be, but I have never found those words.

for Mark

Contents

I

The Falling Sickness	1
Complacent Neurons	2
Cognitive Dysfunction	3
Aura	5
What Happens	6
The Rabbit Hole	7
A Bruised Light	8
Letting Go	9
A Lost Song	10
In media res	11
The Voice of Authority	12

II

Van Gogh: "Wheat Field with Cypress"	15
Van Gogh: "The Starry Night"	16
Van Gogh: "Self Portrait with Palette"	17
Delacroix: "Notes for the Algerian Women in their Harem"	18
Delacroix: "Dante and Virgil in the Infernal Regions"	20
Tasso: "Rinaldo and Armida Observed by Ubaldo and Carlo" by Giambattista Tiepolo	23
Swinburne: The Love of Pain	25
Flaubert: My Attack of Nerves	26
Flaubert: A Writer of Rare Merit	27
Flaubert: The Big Boy, the Bear	28

Lewis Carroll: A Portrait of Alice	30
Dostoyevsky: I Went Flying	31
Strindberg: Alchemy	33
Peter the Great: Traveling Incognito	34
Napoleon: The Retreat	35
Caligula: History's Great Epileptic Leaders	36
Edward Lear: Nonsense Limericks	37
Alfred Lord Tennyson: A Domestic Portrait	39
Schumann: Heaven and Hell	41
Cecilia Ferrazzi: Inquisitorial Testimony	43
Muhammad: The Revelation	45
St. Teresa of Avila: The Blood	46
St. Teresa of Avila: The Body	47

III

Ancient Greek Remedies for Epilepsy	51
Early Christian Cures for Epilepsy	53
Lia Lee: A Hmong Girl in America	55
St. Hildegard of Bingen: Meticulous Visions	57
St. Hildegard of Bingen: One World	59
Dostoyevsky: Morbus Divinus	61

I

The Falling Sickness

Some nights my dreams cross the border
like immigrants desperate to escape
a hungry life. I lick my lips
with words that cannot escape.
My fingers knead my pants
as if they were the finest cashmere,
but I feel only a bleached stillness,
a stiffly woven waiting.
The air is vibrating in a cicada's buzz,
and I cannot hear, I cannot speak
the terror of falling into death –
and then waking
without remembering those last moments,
this hunger for life.

Complacent Neurons

This brain is a sieve where mind
and memory slip away and are lost
when the pills are swallowed
so the seizures don't start
and the neurons stay complacent
as fish in an aquarium.
The misunderstandings are not
understood until later
when the arguments begin.
From the outside, the face has not
changed, the lips still mouth the words
they can remember. Circumambulate,
seditious, ambidextrous,
such slick syllables surface quickly,
float easily to the tongue.
Dishwasher, roller-blade, trolley car
are only pictures, perfectly seen, without text.
When the clothes dryer trips
the circuit, I reset the clocks
to different times. Today
my circuits are askew. I cannot
tell time. Subtraction
becomes addition, but what remains
is simply loss.

Cognitive Dysfunction

...once there was a night in which our failures
became stars we could choose to acknowledge
or abandon.
　　　　　— Marcia Southwick, "The Vanishing Street"

The hardest part is ignoring the constellations,
the failures glowing in minute detail
through memory's latest telescope.
(Where is science when you need her?
Where is medicine now?)
Orion, Andromeda, Cassiopeia,
The Big Dipper, The Little Dipper, yes,
every misspoken word, every
repeated error grows luminous
as a nova in a forgotten sky.
The mouthed mistakes hopscotch
through neuron patterns
linked by faulty logic:
east is west, black is white,
asparagus is artichoke.
The antonyms are all reversed,
the synonyms are not the same.

The stories do not start or end.
Once I wanted to study philosophy,
now I must think carefully
to give directions to get home.
The time has come
to abandon the stars and the sky.
The time has come
to explore the earth beneath my feet.

Aura

Breath wells up inside me
ready to pant my heart
throbs the fear of stopping
time the furniture glowing
your face a halo beside
the lamp of an ordinary
night my limbs tingling
my fingers touching a texture
that cannot be seen
your arms a hollow
shell I am echoing within
a bright distant place
I will leave behind
when the light fails.

What Happens

What happens when button and zipper
have nothing in common and the bus
arrives on the wrong side of the street.
What happens when the lights blink
an unfailing rhythm and sleep
dissolves, salt for a bad dream.
What happens when memory remains
in the next room and letters shift
themselves on a printed page and
the numbers have forgotten how
to count.

The Rabbit Hole

The floor is sinking if floors can sink,
or is it that I am rising like a balloon?
The ground is certainly a long way down.
There should be oxen plowing the fields,
but tile and grout aren't plowed.
My neck is stretching like a rubber band.
When I pop back, will my chin bounce on the ground?
It would not do to have a ball for a head.
I am falling upside down or rather
right side up, but can one fall up?
My, the air is growing black and thin.
How silent is this hole, how dark.
If only this were a curious, curious dream.

A Bruised Light

There is a bruised light at dusk
that is like the aura before
an epileptic seizure. A moment
when the hands held out before
the self do not belong,
but they are still familiar.

There is a moment
when the flickering rhythm
of fan blades above a light
is like a helicopter
ready to land in the brain,
blow the daily sensibilities away.

Eyes averted, hands hidden,
breaths taken, today the moments pass.
Conversation continues around me,
and I join in.

Letting Go

~to Mark Strand~

I would give up my fingers which like a woodpecker tap letters into words.
I would give up my arms which my shoulders have forgotten how to carry.
I would give up my clavicle, a beautiful necklace for jewels to be inset.
I would give up my breasts which have never grown heavy with milk.
I would give up my wide hips, my thighs spreading to flesh, without regret.
I would give up my feet which have climbed ruins, crossed continents.
I would give up my breath which is quiet at night.
I would give up my kidneys which believe stones belong to the earth.
I would give up my uterus which still knows the meaning
   of bleeding and resurrection.
I would not give up my heart,
but I would forswear my tears
for a brain not overcome with chaos theory.
Yet there can be no juggling of organs, no trading of limbs.
I must give up the brain I knew,
begin again with a slower self,
find forgiveness for an ordinary mind.

A Lost Song

In that scream everything human seems obliterated....
It seems indeed as though it were someone else screaming from within.
            —Fyodor Mikhailovich Dostoyevsky, *The Idiot*

I forget the words of the voice
that whispers foreign dreams.
I tell you: Help me remember,
remember...the words tangle, the silence
comes and then the scream, the head
turning to see what is not there,
the muscles clenching, the body falls.

Once I knew the first terror,
I told it: Be quiet. Be quiet.
And it listened. For myself, I said:
This is not fear, only the brain
striking a chord, singing a cappella
for no reason. Yet what is fear
if not this wild song
before the scream begins.

In medias res

Colors press so close
nothing else to see, nothing else,
the terror of colors
droning in the ear.
No breath left,
ready to slip away,
one more minute,
one more minute.

The ceiling, my bedroom.
Hyperventilating.
One slower breath. Another.
Crawl across the carpet.
Push open the door.
Cry out.
His frightened face.
A towel wiping the saliva away.
Blood in the mouth.
Swallow the pills.

My tongue with its edges
now scalloped
like a sea creature,
split again.

The Voice of Authority

The neurons are slow today,
the paintings on the wall silent.

I do what I can do,
pull out pen and paper,
describe what I see:
The blind-folded girl holds two fingers out,
a ledge for the cherub's foot.
A sickle floats behind them.

Then I wait for the words
to start speaking in my head.
The art critic, waiting
for knowledge to descend
like some ancient god of neurology.

Suddenly I see the cherub
is standing on the sickle
like Christ and the girl,
who is painted as a miniature adult
in the Spanish Baroque style,
is a symbol for faith,
blind faith.

II

Van Gogh: "Wheat Field with Cypress"

And the blue sky never tires me....
And the cypress is always occupying my thoughts.
*   —Vincent Van Gogh*

This new attack came over me in the fields
when I was in the midst of painting.
The tips of the cypresses swayed
like flames in the fire but quietly.
And the clouds stopped for only a moment
before the wind swept them away,
and the olive trees were silver, silver
shifting to green like the sky, the sky
that day was mint green, the mountains blue.
Oh, my dear Theo, if only you could have seen
the black splash of the cypress
against the blue, no, in the blue,
and the wheat as golden as the sunset.

I will send you the canvas.
I finished it in spite of everything.

Van Gogh: "The Starry Night"

That does not prevent my having a terrible need of – shall I say the word? – religion.
 —Vincent Van Gogh

The sky roils into stars
that pulse in the night.
The crescent moon holds its halo to itself.
The cypresses grow flames of leaves
to stoke the sky.
The wave of night sweeps over the town,
dyeing the blue ground,
drawing the rows of trees
into foam before the mountains crash
over the tiny, lighted houses,
the thin church spire smaller than a single cypress leaf.

Van Gogh: "Self-Portrait with Palette"

Grief must not gather in our hearts like water in a swamp.
—Vincent Van Gogh

I was thin and pale as a ghost after this last attack,
but I began a portrait the day I got up.
There is no one but myself to paint,
and you know I must paint from what I see.
Those young painters who draw from memory
what do they see of the light or life.

The face is whitish with yellow
and a green cast, the cheeks gaunt.
The air is a dark violet-blue
as if the mirror had drawn the night inside.
Do not worry, my brother,
I am almost myself again,
and work is the best remedy.

Delacroix: Notes for "The Algerian Women in their Harem"

This preparation of Prussian blue, vermilion *and* white *can also be used for flesh where the half-tint is violet.... Where the half-tint is green, on the other hand, the preparation should be composed of* raw umber *and* white, *or some other green tone.*
—Eugene Delacroix

Kohl on the edges of their eyelids; eyes almond shaped. Eyebrows a stroke of black. One looking down, a black scarf wrapped around her neck like hair falling over her shoulder.

Patterns everywhere. Floor tiles in six-sided stars. Rugs woven; reds predominate. Diamond shapes, lines, triangles, all in rows. One rug with wide, brown and beige stripes. Cushion beige; red and black abstract design. Arabic calligraphy is painted on the wall inside a painted picture frame. Wall across the room tiled, geometric shapes. The wall in shadows receding into darkness.

Three women sitting on the floor. One in the foreground lounging on the beige cushion. One sitting with crossed legs. One holding the tube of a water pipe.

Each with three rings on three fingers on both hands. Pearl chokers around their necks. A single jewel dangles from two strands. Thin gold circles for bracelets, ankle rings.

Blouses loose and short sleeved above plump, sensuous arms. Shadows cast beneath the sleeves. Vests clasped just below the bosom. Each skirt in different patterns and colors. One blue flowered; one green with gold trim; the other white, glowing in the light. Cloth crumpled to reveal harem pants; length mid-calf. Bare feet. Slippers scattered about.

Their eyes must look away as though they don't see a man in the harem or later the beholder in the museum. Quiet faces. A lovely moment of repose. Except for the black servant. Red and black skirt knotted at her hips. White blouse, brown vest but plain.

She looks back; her body twisting at the waist. Deep brown arm held in the air. Her foot caught in mid-step, her heel frozen above the floor. Her right arm almost touching the picture edge. She is walking away from this richness, this hidden beauty.

Delacroix: "Dante and Virgil in the Infernal Regions"

Beneath the water there are people bereft
who exhale such sighs they fill the pond with froth.
See the water bubbles with their breath.
　　　　　　　—Dante Alighieri, *Inferno*

Gnawing the wood, their desperation growing,
the damned struggle to climb aboard the boat,
their hopeless eyes closed or like coals glowing,

the sparks from fires that never burn out,
an air without sun, the clouds only smoke.
One body's flesh floating, his eyes about

to open, to see his skin again soaked
with the blood flowing from his pale chest split
open by a serpent's fangs, his ribs broken.

Death and rebirth, the cycle perverted
by one of many unfathomable
agonies of body and mind: heads twisted

around and deprived of forward sight, able
to walk only onwards through backwards lives.
Everywhere there is a moaning rabble.

These torments are cast on all who lived
outside the laws of Christianity.
Each circle descends by greater evil.

First those unbaptized in antiquity.
Next the carnal sinners, gluttons, misers.
Heresy, murder, thievery, sorcery –

All just a preface to the worst traitors
who betrayed God and men, wallowed in sin.
The tormentor and tormented – Lucifer –

with three heads and three jaws shreds the skin
of Judas, Brutus, Cassius, then bites,
chews, grinds them each again and again.

Beyond them is the path into the bright
realms, the stars, purgatory, paradise,
but Dante cannot imagine these sights

as he crosses the Styx with Virgil, his eyes
filled with terror of what he will find,
of how his own soul can ever suffice.

It is only when he sees the signs
of death in life can he leave both behind.

Tasso: "Rinaldo and Armida Observed
  by Ubaldo and Carlo"
    by Giambattista Tiepolo

So deeply now he sighs, it makes you think,
'His soul is now becoming her soul.'
    — Torquato Tasso, *Jerusalem Delivered*

A bed of forest velvet
with silken sheets
    floating
in a breeze that sent
Cupid tumbling.
Armida's breast bared
for a hand to stroke.
Her rumpled blouse
a vestige of dress.

Rinaldo gazed into her eyes
and spoke of stars,
the tiny mirrors
of her sweet face.
In the glass, she saw herself
lost in love.

Behind a wall,
two soldiers waited
for the witch to leave,
to claim Rinaldo as leader
of the last Crusade
for the Holy City of Jerusalem.

First, their lascivious eyes looked
at her breasts, her thighs,
this moment of love undressed.

Swinburne: The Love of Pain

By the lips intertwisted and bitten
 Till the foam has a savour of blood...
I adjure thee, respond from thy altars,
 Our Lady of Pain.
   —Algernon Charles Swinburne, "Dolores"

Languorous eyelids, lips
to be bitten,
skin striped
with the switch's red strikes –
luxuries for a poet
proclaiming de Sade,
Baudelaire and slipping
into the cesspool.

Little, pigeon-chested man,
carrot hair bleached by drink,
limbs always jumping
like St. Vitus at the dance,
prepare to tumble down
and be carried out corpse-like
to the countryside,
face chalked, head bleeding,
nursed and reformed again,
still the Admiral's drunken child at 31.

Flaubert: My Attack of Nerves

I feel the breath cross my face.
I have a flame in my left eye.
I see yellow, everywhere, yellow.

The quinine, the bleeding and purging, the leeches,
they do nothing. Even the thread
drawn through the skin of my neck does nothing.

The burning water Father poured over my hand
has shriveled the skin like that of a mummy.
My fingers feel little heat or cold.

Each day before my eyes I see strands of hair,
crumpled like those pulled from a woman's comb.
My nerves quiver, my stomach trembles.

With this illness, I can spend my time as I wish, writing,
but good food, wine, tobacco, without these
I am a dead man.

Flaubert: A Writer of Rare Merit

Epilepsy, the great nerve storm, that which Paracelsus has called the earthquake of man's moral being, had struck Gustave and had laid him low.
—Maxime Du Camp

His was a ghost's face, lit only
by the flame of anguish in his eye.
He waited, then knew to walk across the room
and throw his body on the bed.
His mouth spoke words he would forget:
"I am holding the reins, the cart is coming,
I hear the tinkling of bells. Ah!
I see a lamp at the inn."
A writer of genius died that night
on the road from Pont-Audemer to Rouen
when his first cry seared the air
and he became convulsed.

His mind was arrested and then he wrote only
what he knew at age 22 as, indeed, others have.
His faithful memory failed him.
He thought it was the quinine cure.
He spent days writing a single phrase.
Strangely, he knew the end of his sentences,
the timbre of the words,
before he ever wrote their beginnings.

Flaubert: The Big Boy, the Bear

*He is a man who saw something killed before his eyes in his lifetime:
an illusion, a dream, I cannot tell which.*
—Edmund and Jules de Goncourt

The big boy is vulgarly happy –
blue bulging eyes penetrating through,
Manchurian mustaches and a trumpet's voice,
his brick-red face ravaged by pox.
He has suffered more, lived more than anyone before.
"One must live as a bourgeois and think as a demigod" –
such tripe.

Tonight the bear read us his manuscript from six to nine,
then dinner and more after.
His words rang out, the theater come home.
Last week his voice was hoarse, his lungs pained
for he yells as he writes, screams every syllable
into the study's still air.

Each word must be exactly right.
One year he wrote only thirteen pages.
But I am afraid of what will come of this book.

He has been writing for two years,
so I dare not speak my mind to my friend.
What a trial to write one's best novel first.

Lewis Carroll: A Portrait of Alice

I envisioned her as the Beggar Child
in tattered skirts and blouse,
her small white shoulders bared
between the tears. She slipped
her shoes off willingly, happily,
but pouted at all the waiting
as I readied the photographic plate,
exposed the picture, counted to 45,
then washed it, watching her lovely face
rise from the darkness that stained my hands.

Dostoyevsky: I Went Flying

The fear of death is now beginning to pass, but it is still extreme, so I dare not lie down.
         —Fyodor Mikhailovich Dostoyevsky

1. 18 July 1849

The floor was heaving, trying to catch its breath.
A peacock was stifled in my throat,
and I am told my face turned blue.
I did not know to watch for the moon.

2. 29 January 1870

At three a.m. I fell when walking down the hall.
When I rose, I carried a candle in the darkness
without knowing if it was light or dark,
waking or sleeping, my feet moving
beneath the half moon without me.

3. 8 April 1875

I went flying while walking across the room
and awoke sitting on the floor, pen in hand.
I rolled four cigarettes, not accurately,

then drank three glasses of water in one gulp.
The moon was just full, and for a long time
I could not understand what had happened.

4. 8 April 1881

Today I will have a lethargic sleep.
Watch even for the faintest fog on a mirror
held before my face. Listen,
my brother, listen closely at my chest.
The new moon approaches.
Do not bury me for seven days.

Strindberg: Alchemy

When I awoke, something was leading me on,
letters I could almost see. A formula for love,
for alchemy, a choice, a strange dream.
I walked to the Gare Montparnasse without knowing
which train I should take or when.
I sat down and waited. I knew I would know.
I remembered the walnut that sprouted
two tiny hands clasped in quiet white prayer,
and then a woman sat down beside me
and pulled off her white gloves and beneath
were her white hands. I knew
she would lead me to knowledge from the hand of the Unseen.
When she boarded the train to Meudon, I followed.
I walked up the main street, turned down an alley.
Two letters were drawn on a wall: "F" and "S."
Her initials! Frida still loved me!
The divorce, my stupidity. She would forgive me.
Then an "e" appeared: "Fe" and "S." Iron and sulphur.
The secret for gold! I had the formula for gold.
But Frida would not have me as a scientist.
My life as a writer was over.
Science was what remained.

Peter the Great: Traveling Incognito

He calls himself Peter Mikhailov
and lives among the shipwrights,
eating as we do, learning the carpenter's trade.
His hands are rough from the ax and the lathe,
his shoulders thin for the weight he can lift.
He wears no court wig, but his eyes
are the eyes of a man who has sent soldiers to die
and watched traitors knouted,
their bones broken on the wheel,
the ax taken to their necks.
You will know him by his great height,
the wart on the right side of his face,
and the shaking and twitching of his left arm and face.

Napoleon: The Retreat

Once he stopped a court procession.
He didn't fall frothing at the mouth that day,
just stared as though there were something
to be seen where there was nothing.
His courtiers encircled him,
hiding the statue Napoleon from view.
When he came to and saw the circle of faces,
he sputtered, What were they all doing?
Why had they stopped here?
And he strutted onward –
toward Waterloo and that final battle
where he would retreat, enclosed by a square
of Grenadiers, a battalion of the Old Guard.

Caligula: History's Great Epileptic Leaders

What was Caesar compared to me?
I owe my blood to Julius,
but was he a God?
No. I am the first Caesar
to converse with Jove.

Julius invaded Brittanicus
but was it not lost
and left for me to claim again?
A triumphant battle,
my ship alone
slicing the Channel.
For my soldiers
I provided the spoils of the sea –
helmets full of shells.
For our victory,
for me, their God,
a lighthouse was built,
a lighthouse greater than that
of Pharos at Alexandria
for Alexander was nothing
compared to me.

Edward Lear: Nonsense Limericks

1

There was an Old Man of Athens
Who forgot his red paints and black pens,
    So he drew with his nose
      While the wind blew the rose;
Thus he smelt no flowers in Athens.

There was a Young Painter in Turkey
Who wanted to paint what he could see,
    But an old man said no,
      Wagging his finger so;
Then he poured the Painter some mint tea.

A Foolish Man who swam up the Nile
Saw six pelicans in the first mile.
    Then plovers, pigeons, crane,
      Hawks and eagles fell like rain
And swam beside the Man single file.

2

There was an Old Demon of Highgate
Who had knocked at the door of a pate
    To whisper in the ear
    Of a boy called Lear
Who believed the Demon was his fate.

Lear was hoping to sell a painting
When the Count came in and stood waiting;
    Waving his money
    He looked quite funny
Until the Count paid for a painting.

Lear read today that Old Fortescue
Would live in a Cabinet too.
    He bounced up in a swish
    And tossed up a small fish;
Its tail flew off for old Fortescue.

Alfred Lord Tennyson: A Domestic Portrait

"...seeing either sex alone
Is half itself, and in true marriage lies
Nor equal, nor unequal: each fulfills
Defect in each...."
          —Alfred Lord Tennyson

EMILY'S JOURNAL ENTRIES, 1856

January
6th. Hallam loves the stars. Every night
he wants to see his brother Lionel's namesake,
but I tell him
he will have to wait until spring
to see the Lion.

February
14th. A. reads me *Romeo & Juliet*.
15th. *Hamlet* & *Richard III*.
A. remarked upon the contrast.

March
12th. I heard the first Stock dove in the elm.
30th. Mr. & Mrs. Cameron come for dinner.
Julia is planning a portrait soon.
A. reads "Merlin" & "Maud."

April
20th. A. troubled about the *Idylls*.
I think he will recall the proofs
& not publish the book.
23rd. We weed the garden, which is easy
after a light rain.

Schumann: Heaven and Hell

It is the inner hearing of wondrously beautiful pieces of music, fully formed and complete!
    —Robert Schumann

1. 17th February 1854

Clara, the angels' music speaks in melody.
I understand it perfectly:
We will be in Heaven within the year.
I need pen and ink to write the notes.
How lovely, how lovely, look.

2. 18th February 1854

Clara, tigers are dragging me to Hell.
Hyenas are shrieking my sins,
my ears will burst with their demonic opera.
Save me, save me!

3. 26ᵗʰ February 1854

Clara, I am afraid for you,
afraid of what I might do in the night.
You must send me to the asylum.
I have packed my bags.
I will come back soon, recovered,
and we will play my angelic themes.

On 27 February 1854, Robert Schumann attempted suicide by drowning. On 4 March, his wife, Clara, reluctantly hospitalized him in a private asylum in Edenich, Germany. Schumann died there in 1856 of self-starvation at the age of 46.

Cecilia Ferrazzi: Inquisitorial Testimony

In the name of the Lord and of His Mother, the Most Holy Virgin Mary.
On 9 July 1664, in the prison of the Holy Inquisition of Venice.
I, Cecilia Ferrazzi, depose as the truth the things written below.

1

The faints and fits began when I was five,
and to ease the convulsions, my mother
dressed me in dark blue, the color of St. Valentine.
When I was six, I grew my second set of teeth.
Even then I saw a beautiful woman
wearing a glowing dress, whispering that these
were the pains I must suffer for God.

2

When I was older, the Devil began knocking on my door.
Sometimes he was an animal
or a horrible man breathing fire,
beating me bloody with clubs and rods of iron.
Afterwards I went into a rapture
and the Mother of God collected the blood
which she said would bloom into roses
as the drops fell from her hands to the earth.

3

Once I saw a large crucifix moving
and then disappearing on the street.
Inside the church I saw another cross
adorned with gems and still another appeared
covered with spines and stumps, and a voice
asked from within which of the two I would choose,
and I said, "Lord, give me the one
with the spines and stumps that I may serve you."
And I hugged it to my breast and felt great joy
when I emerged from my trance.

Cecilia Ferrazzi was convicted of "the pretense of sanctity" by the Venetian Inquisition on 1 September 1665. She served seven years in jail and was prohibited from ever again speaking of any divine favors supposedly shown her. She died in 1684 at the age of 74.

Muhammad: The Revelation

Gabriel spoke – in the name of God,
the most compassionate, the most merciful –
the Archangel spoke
and smote me on the head with scripture.
In that moment,
the first of the words of God
rushed into my head,
letters for me, who cannot read, to read,
blinding stars to illumine the dark cave.

Frightened, I ran home,
then fell down in a fit.
I could not believe I was called
to be the messenger of God.

St. Teresa of Avila: The Blood

After this prayer of union, the soul is left with a great tenderness.
—St. Teresa of Avila

How dry is my soul, my mouth before the blood.
After Communion on Palm Sunday last,
my soul hovered outside me,
longing to be one tongue praising God.

When I came back to myself,
the body of Christ was still dissolving on my tongue
and my mouth was filled with blood,
such an exquisite sweetness, and the Lord said,
"Daughter, I want my blood to do you good."

My soul, my poor, wretched, evil soul,
is not worthy of this purification, this pain.

St. Teresa of Avila: The Body

A humble and a contrite heart, Oh Lord, thou wilt not despise.
—The last prayer of St. Teresa of Avila

Her feet when I kissed them were a brilliant white,
a smell of flowers rose from the skin.
That night a haunting fragrance
filled the convent and the air was bright
with memories, the fiery wings of moths
burnt at the candle flames beside her bed.

Later they broke the mortar and stone
to remove her body from the crypt
meant to hold her for all eternity.
There was no stench of corruption.
That sweet scent still touched her shriveled skin.
She was perfect, only her nose was broken by the coffin lid.
Soon she was in parts – a hand, an arm, a rib –
to ease the pain of dying, the life of pain.

Later a charred hole was found in her heart,
a sign of her rapture and the angel
who had plunged the tip of a golden spear,
flaming into her breathing heart.
Later still that heart grew a circle of thorns,
a tribute to the Sacred Heart of Jesus Christ.

III

Ancient Greek Remedies for Epilepsy

Wear an amulet of stones
found in the stomachs of swallows at the waxing moon.

Walk a straight route where perfume fills the air.

Anoint the neck with vinegar and rose oil,
the limbs with olive oil.

Breathe spices to provoke sneezing before going to bed.

Drink vinegar diluted with honey,
add the juice of squills – this will work in 40 days.

Eat not the eel or goat, the deer or pig,
mint, garlic or the onion that brings death.

Avoid the clothes of mourning
and never cross your hands or feet.

Eat part of the liver of a gladiator nine times
or better still drink his blood as it foams warm from his veins,
suck his soul from his wounds.

Try bloodletting, vomiting and purging.

Eat the flesh of a wild beast killed
with an iron weapon that once killed a man.

Mix a medicine of the feces of a land crocodile,
the heart and genitals of a hare,
the blood of a sea tortoise
and the testicles of a boar, or you may use a ram.

If all these fail, have an iron nail
driven into your skull marking the place
where your head first struck the ground.

Yet if you vomit a drink of acacia,
there is nothing to be done.
The sacred disease will plague you all of your life.

Early Christian Cures for Epilepsy

And as he is who falls, and knows not how,
By forces of demons who to earth drag him down.
          —Dante Alighieri, *Inferno*

Cut the patient's little finger and write in his blood
the three names – Jasper, Melchior, Balthazar.
Place gold, frankincense and myrrh in a box.
Instruct him to say three Ave Marias and three Pater Nosters
for the souls of the fathers and mothers of the three kings.
Have him drink of the juice of the peony –
mixed with beer or wine – have him drink this
for 30 days, say the prayers each day three times
for the three fathers and the three mothers,
and he shall be cured of the falling evil.

Take the epileptic or the lunatic or the demoniac
to mass on the Friday and Saturday
of the second week past Whitsunday.
Keep him from the Eucharist
that he not desecrate the common cup and plate.
Beware of the contagion from his evil breath.

On Sunday let the priest write the words of the Gospel
that Jesus spoke to raise the child from his fit,
"This kind of demon is not cast out but by prayer,"
and the man possessed shall be healed.

Lia Lee: A Hmong Girl in America

The doctors can fix some sicknesses that involve the body and the blood, but for us Hmong, some people get sick because of their soul and they need spiritual things.
— Nao Kao Lee

1

The spoon rubbed on the skin,
the coin inside the boiled, black egg
inside the cloth rubbed on the skin
have not stopped the tightening
of the limbs,
the blue lips, the stopped
breath. The pig
sacrificed to bring
the lost soul home,
the chickens, the cow,
none are enough.

2

Phenobarbital, Tegretol,
Depakene (Depakote),
a Western litany begun
too late, too little,
too much.

The needle desperate
for a vein
cannot stop the clock
of the arching limbs,
cannot keep the brain
from losing its way.

Foua Yang and Nao Kao Lee are Hmong refugees who left Laos with their family in 1980 in the aftermath of the CIA-sponsored war in Laos. Lia, their 14th child, was born in California in 1982. She began having grand-mal seizures when she was three months old. In *The Spirit Catches You and You Fall Down: A Hmong Child, Her American Doctors and the Collision of Two Cultures,* Anne Fadiman tells the complex and tragic story of how Lia ended up severely brain damaged at age four, due to seizures.

St. Hildegard of Bingen: Meticulous Visions

The heavens were opened and a blinding light of exceptional brilliance flowed through my entire brain.
—St. Hildegard of Bingen

Man stands
in the circles of fire,
water, ether and air.
His arms and toes stretch
towards the crab of trust,
the stag of faith,
the leopard of fear
and the wolf of hell,
their breaths stroking his skin.

Above, seven planets circle,
sixteen stars turn,
a vision of the seven gifts
of the Holy Spirit
and the sixteen teachers
of the six eras
of human history.

An exact memory
of wheel and stars:
divine visions,
translations,
all sanctioned
by Pope Eugenius
from the very beginning.

St. Hildegard of Bingen: One World

I saw a mysterious and wonderful vision so that my inmost core was convulsed and I lost all bodily sensation, as my knowledge was altered to another mode, unknown to myself.
—St. Hildegard of Bingen

1

The moon is the clock
of the seasons,
as the stars are blessed
with reason
seen in their movements
through the sky.

2

Grass is the earth's
soft skin,
rocks are its bones
of fire,
soil
its green marrow.

3

The humors of the body
leap like leopards,
parch the liver,
consume the marrow
of human bones
to cause seizures
as the moon wanes.

Dostoyevsky: Morbus Divinus

I felt that heaven had descended to earth and swallowed me.
—Fyodor Mikhailovich Dostoyevsky

While I was sleeping, the moon split into shards,
its crescent repeated three times, three months
passing in a single flash of light.
My nervous tongue spoke a foreign language,
my eyes read the calligraphy of crescents,
a Biblical verse proclaiming, "Da. Da."
Yes, yes, the glow spread from east to west.
Now there shall be no more time.
No time to be cast out of the blue sky.
No time for disbelief in devils.
No time for mourning the dead.
For this moment, this ecstasy before the darkness,
I would give up my very life.

Morbus divinus ("death divine" in Latin) refers to the ancient concept of epilepsy as a transcendent, religious experience.

Notes

"Van Gogh: 'Wheat Field with Cypress'": The poem draws on several of Van Gogh's letters to his brother Theo. The first two lines are paraphrased and the last two lines are quoted from one of the letters, which are collected in *Dear Theo: The Autobiography of Vincent Van Gogh*, edited by Irving Stone with Jean Stone.

"Van Gogh: 'Self-Portrait with Palette'": "I was thin and pale as a ghost" is quoted from one of Van Gogh's letters to his brother Theo.

"Flaubert: My Attack of Nerves": Before having a seizure, Flaubert would say, "I have a flame in my left eye," according to Maxime Du Camp, one of Flaubert's friends. The last two lines of the poem are paraphrased from Flaubert. The source for both is *Flaubert: A Biography* by Herbert Lottman.

"Flaubert: A Writer of Rare Merit": The quotation "I am holding the reins …" is by Flaubert, according to Maxine Du Camp, who also called Flaubert "a writer of rare merit" in his *Souvenirs Littéraires*.

"Flaubert: The Big Boy, the Bear": The quotation "One must live as a bourgeois…" is by Flaubert (from Lottman).

"Dostoyevsky: I Went Flying": The poem's second journal entry is based on Dostoyevsky's Jan. 29, 1870 journal entry. The poem's fourth journal entry quotes Dostoyevsky's brother Andrei who wrote that Dostoyevsky would leave notes saying "Today I will have a lethargic sleep, so do not bury me for (such-and-such) days." Both of these sources appear in James L. Rice's *Doestoevsky and the Healing Art: An Essay in Literary and Medical History*.

"St. Teresa of Avila" The Blood": "Daughter, I want my blood to do you good" is a quotation from St. Teresa of words spoken to her by God when she emerged from what she called a "state of suspension" (from *Teresa: A Woman* by Victoria Lincoln).

"Ancient Greek Remedies" and "Early Christian Cures for Epilepsy": Many of these treatments are drawn from Owsei Tempkin's *The Falling Sickness: A History of Epilepsy from the Greeks to the Beginnings of Modern Neurology*. The first Christian cure that involves the three wise men is attributed to John of Ardene.

Acknowledgments

I would like to thank the Arizona Commission on the Arts for a project award that enabled me to begin this work.

I am grateful to Steven Swerdfeger, my publisher, for his appreciation of *A Bruised Light* and for his commitment to publishing it. A special thank you goes to Cynthia Hogue whose longtime support for my poetry made the publication of this book possible in a very real way. Thank you to Hoge Day for his friendship and for the beautiful artwork that graces the cover of this collection. Most importantly, thank you to my husband, Mark Taylor, for his love and support through the hard years and through the truly wonderful ones, too.

PAMELA PORTWOOD received a project award from the Arizona Commission on the Arts in support of writing *A Bruised Light*. Her poetry has been published in *Borderlands, Toronto Review of Contemporary Writing Abroad, Visions International, Apalachee Quarterly, Earth's Daughters* and other periodicals. Her poems also have appeared in the anthologies *Life on the Line, Women and Death* and *This Far Together: Haight Ashbury Literary Journal Anthology*. She worked as a free-lance writer and art critic for over 15 years, and her art columns were carried by *The Arizona Daily Star* (Tucson), the *Tucson Weekly* and *Artspace* (Albuquerque, N.M.). She also received a fellowship in art criticism from the National Gallery of Art. In 2005, after completing an Associate of Arts' degree in interior design at The Art Center Design College, she embarked on a new career as an interior designer. Portwood holds a Master of Fine Arts' degree in creative writing from the University of Arizona. She lives in Tucson, Arizona with her husband, Mark Taylor.

www.ingramcontent.com/pod-product-compliance
Lightning Source LLC
Chambersburg PA
CBHW030004050426
42451CB00006B/114